ENTREPRENEURSHIP
THE WRIGHT WAY

Your Ultimate Guide to Becoming a Successful Entrepreneur Right Away!

GWENNETTA WRIGHT

"Entrepreneurship the Wright Way
Your Ultimate Guide to Becoming a Successful Entrepreneur Right Away"

Copyright © 2016 Gwennetta Wright
All Rights Reserved

The information included in this book is for educational purposes only. The author and publisher have made best efforts to ensure the information in this book is accurate. However, they make no warranties as to the accuracy or completeness of the contents herein, and cannot be held responsible for any errors, omissions, or dated material.

This book is geared toward providing exact and reliable information in regards to the topics and issues covered. The publication is sold with the idea that the publisher is not required to render accounting, officially permitted, or otherwise, qualified services. If advice is necessary, legal or professional, a practiced individual in the profession should be ordered.

Liability Disclaimer:
By reading this book, you assume all risks associated with using the advice, data and suggestions given below, with a full understanding that you, solely, are responsible for anything that may occur as a result of putting this information into action in any way, and regardless of your interpretation of the advice.

ISBN-13: 9781537573724
ISBN-10: 1537573721

ENTREPRENEURSHIP
THE WRIGHT WAY

Your Ultimate Guide to Becoming a Successful
Entrepreneur Right Away!

Table of Contents

What This Book Has For You I

Introduction: Believe in the Entrepreneur Inside You 1

Chapter 1: Understanding Entrepreneurship 3
    Who is an Entrepreneur 5
    Types of Entrepreneurship 7
    Top Reasons to Become an Entrepreneur 11
    Questions that First-Time Entrepreneurs Ask 17

Chapter 2: Establishing Your Entrepreneur Mindset—
    Making the Important Shifts 21
    Why You Need the Right Entrepreneur Mindset 23
    What Makes You Different? The Difference between an
        Entrepreneur Mindset and Employee Mindset 26
    What You Need To Do To Shift the Mindset 30
    Entrepreneurial Development Levels 35

Chapter 3: Write the Vision—Setting Your Goal the Right Way 45
    Setting Up a Business—
        Importance of Setting Goals to Achieve 47
    Why You Should Only Set "SMART" Goals 52
    What Are Vision Boards and How to Use Them
        for Goal Setting 57

A Goal-Supporting System—
    Creating the Right System to Achieve Your Goals 61
Five Important Goals You Should Not Miss Out On
    as an Entrepreneur 63

Chapter 4: Taking Care of Essential Entrepreneurial Aspects:
    Time Management 67
Why Time Management is Critical for Entrepreneurs 69
Benefits You Can Guarantee with Time Management 71
Setting the Right Time Management Plan
    for Your Business 73

Chapter 5: Understanding Core Leadership 77
What is Leadership and how is it Different
    from Entrepreneurship 79
Adopting the Most Important Leadership Qualities to Become
    a Successful Entrepreneur 80

Chapter 6: Team Building—Entrepreneurship Key to Growth 85
The Importance of Working with a Solid Team 87
The Roles and Responsibilities of Team Working 90
Facing the Challenge of Changing Team Members 93
Five Important Habits Every Entrepreneur Should Practice 96

Final Word 99

What This Book Has For You

Everyone's running the same race these days—the race to achieve financial freedom.

Becoming your own boss is nothing less than a dream come true. Reaching your financial turnover point is not impossible if you know what to do. If you think entrepreneurship is what will help you reach your financial freedom, this book is definitely the perfect pick for you.

Statistics show that 7 in 10 small business owners are out of business in less than two years. The reason why so many entrepreneurs fail within the first two years of business is due to poor planning. Usually when a person starts on the journey of entrepreneurship, they are not taught the basic fundamentals of operating a business.

When you decide that you want to explore the opportunity of becoming an entrepreneur, you have to know that it is more than just getting a business name and opening a business bank account. Being an entrepreneur is having the guts to take risks and having the willingness to manage and organize a business venture.

This book includes all of the information that helps you identify the important aspects you need to develop in order to become a successful entrepreneur. The methods revealed here are not rocket-science, but are based more on strategy building and general knowledge related to starting and running a new business that will help you achieve your ultimate goals.

If thinking about it or preparing your mind to start your own business seems like a fearful task to you, then reading this book will give you the information you need to prepare or expand yourself on the journey of entrepreneurship.

Below is a sneak peek of some of the areas that will be discussed in this book:

Introduction to what entrepreneurship is all about—the information will help you identify if you have what it takes to become a successful entrepreneur.

Highlighting areas that help an individual become entrepreneurial; changing of mindset, establishing the right mindset of an entrepreneur, and why doing so is important.

The relationship between successful entrepreneurship and goal setting and why it is important to set SMART goals to achieve them.

Importance of time management for entrepreneurship and how it can be practiced effectively.

Explanation on why building a team is necessary for any new startup business or entrepreneur, and how it can play an integral role in the success of the newly startup business.

Indeed, entrepreneurship is not for everyone; but if you have identified the need to experience freedom and generate some income by becoming your own boss, this book is surely going to help you take the right path. In addition to following the details in the book, making strategies before taking every step, and being able to take some risks is what will make you a successful entrepreneur.

So get started now, and learn how entrepreneurship can change your entire life and perspective. All of the answers you have been looking for are in this book. So read till the end, and get ready to call the shots for your own good.

Good luck!

Introduction:
Believe in the Entrepreneur Inside You

While it is true that not everyone can become an entrepreneur, it is also true that we all have an entrepreneur hidden inside of us. It is we who sometimes fail to identify and accept it.

Entrepreneurship is not just a business, it's a lifestyle that people can learn. It is a mindset that comes from within, and therefore makes each and every one of us capable of becoming a successful entrepreneur. We are born with the ability to make our way through every day's struggle and survive—which generally requires innovative thinking, planning, and strategy making.

We make decisions every now and then. Sometimes they are simple, petty ones with no serious outcomes. At other times, the decision made could be really crucial, and can have a long-lasting impact on your life as a result. Regardless of the type of decision you have to make, you know it is going to have an impact over your life. You take your time to decide and come up with various innovative ideas that help you make up your mind, move on, or adapt to a challenging situation.

Just like entrepreneurship, our daily living also requires decision making. After taking all the relevant considerations into account, we choose to make a decision and accept the results it brings with it. When we are involved in this process multiple times on a daily basis, we don't realize we are actually engaged in an act of practical entrepreneurship.

In simple words, being entrepreneurial is exactly this—thinking about and acting upon something that requires decision-making (and probably something that we have never done before) in order to achieve a certain outcome or desirable goal. Just like our lives, entrepreneurship is also about addressing and assessing situations, using innovative ideas and mindset to design various alternatives, and then keeping all the important factors into account to choose a new way—and even multiple ways as a combination—to find the most suitable solution that hopefully leads us to something better.

Of course, even in real life, we seem to put our own benefits and interests first.

If that sounds like you, you definitely have an entrepreneur hidden inside you too. So it's time to unleash it and see what success has in stock for you as a great entrepreneur.

Chapter 1

Understanding Entrepreneurship

Entrepreneurship is different from simply owning a business. There is much more to entrepreneurship that makes you a successful business person. That's why it is highly important that you learn about entrepreneurship and the reason why you want to travel on this journey.

Who is an Entrepreneur

You may be a business owner, but that does not make you an entrepreneur. You need many more qualities to call yourself a successful entrepreneur who is aware of all the tactics to take their business to the next level.

So who exactly is an entrepreneur?

An entrepreneur is an initiator. He or she is someone who is ready to take the challenge and has the courage to keep the risks aside and take the initiative to set up a business. An entrepreneur is the beginning as well as the end of an activity, project or a venture.

An entrepreneur may or may not be the one behind the idea, but they are definitely the person who takes up the drive to change that idea into a reality.

An entrepreneur is the person in charge of the activities. He or she is not only responsible for establishing or initiating the project, they are also responsible for taking the lead to continue with activities that run the business. An entrepreneur is the leader who takes the first step and sets the example for the team and inspires them to follow the same path.

He or she has taken responsibility of the driver's seat and takes the control to accelerate, change direction, slow down, take a turn, or even put the brakes on the venture.

An entrepreneur is in all means responsible and accountable throughout the journey. If you are only setting up a business and are not participating or taking charge in how it is operated, you might also want to give up the authorities and the rights toward responsibilities that come with it. Being an entrepreneur, the business and everything associated with it is your responsibility. You are accountable for the activities and operations carried out by the business, and the person ultimately responsible for the destiny of the venture.

In simple words, being an entrepreneur, you have the highest stakes in the business venture, and therefore it naturally falls as your responsibility to fully direct the endeavor.

A successful entrepreneur is able to see an opportunity in every type of situation. He or she has the ability to figure out the way that opportunity can be utilized in the most resourceful manner to turn it into a reward.

When you think about entrepreneurship, you often end up imagining a successful, fast-growing business that started with a very small team and grew up with a lot of hard work and dedication. While this is a great example of entrepreneurship, it is not limited to this definition. Entrepreneurship is a very vast subject that can help individuals, as well as communities and organizations, to change opportunities into actions for increasing or maintaining wellbeing.

Entrepreneurship is much more than just business-related traits and qualities. It is a behavior, which can be found and encouraged in anybody to boost financial, social, and cultural wellbeing. We are all naturally blessed with this quality and are capable of using it for amazing benefits. However, only a few of us are good at taking advantage of every opportunity that knocks, and that's what separates successful entrepreneurs from just entrepreneurs.

Types of Entrepreneurship

What type of entrepreneur are you?

I have classified entrepreneurship into four different types based on how each one operates. Below are details of each type to give you a better understanding of which type of entrepreneur you are.

The One Who Achieves

These people are the goal setters. Their eyes are constantly on the final prize. They do not only want to achieve that goal, but they are the people who set those challenging personal goals for themselves. Entrepreneurs who are achievers are more dedicated than the other types because they are really focused on achieving their ultimate goal. They do not hesitate in investing a lot of hard work, effort, and time to achieve what they have planned.

They are the planners who tend to design the entire pathway that takes them closer to their ultimate goal. They have a very committed attitude toward their goal, and are likely to make things happen their way. They are excellent when it comes to working efficiently during tough times. In short, they are good at everything.

Entrepreneurs who are achievers are focused on running small businesses and taking one step at a time as they continue to gain knowledge. They do not claim or expect to know everything. However, they are designed to follow their own directions, and may not be able to work at a large or highly structured organization that is mostly controlled by third parties.

The One Who Sells

These entrepreneurs are more about people and are more focused on the wellbeing of the community than anything else. They have a natural soft-sell approach to their entrepreneurship method, and their customers are often highly loyal to these entrepreneurs, mainly to show the same gratitude to them as they have received.

This type of entrepreneurs focuses on selling and do not really play an active role in the management. Since their main aim is to provide more to the people and achieve more in terms of sales, they often hire other people to look after and manage their business for them.

The One Who Manages

This type of entrepreneur is totally the opposite of the previous type; they have a more decisive and competitive mindset, and are more focused on their leadership/management role. They have a personality which makes them more comfortable and active when they are in charge of everything.

These entrepreneurs are often expected to do well in other areas of entrepreneurship as well—including sales since they are both persuasive and logical. However, their biggest strength is managing major growth by taking the lead and working on their existing operations or the new organization talents.

With these types of entrepreneurs, it is very important that proper skills are learned, and knowledge has been obtained before they go on and over-manage small or insignificant operations.

They have a more active role to play within the management of the business, and tend to hire other people to take care of the sales and marketing—i.e. by working with a proper sales and marketing team.

The One Who Invents

These types of entrepreneurs are more creative and naturally drawn to finding new ways and coming up with innovative ideas to get ahead of the competition. However, their enthusiasm can work both ways for them—in their favor and against them. Therefore, it is very important that they keep a little charge there and do not let their enthusiasm take over.

Due to their creative approach, they are great at envisioning solutions to keep up with the most challenging tasks for the sake of the organization and its success. They are expected to keep their focus on areas they are already good at. Moreover, it is also important for them to remember that not every idea is going to work in favor of the business, and therefore it is important to carry out a detailed analysis before the ideas are implemented.

Some of you might be able to relate more to one of the types mentioned above, while a majority of you could relate to more than one type; it is possible, since some people actually possess more than one type of entrepreneurship trait in them.

For instance, manager and achiever are traits that are often found in people in a combination. People who possess more traits of entrepreneurship are naturally believed to be more successful entrepreneurs as they have the knowledge, experience, and expertise to handle a number of different types of situations. Now identify your type, and see if you can still relate with only one or more traits and write those traits down.

Top Reasons to Become an Entrepreneur

If you are seriously thinking about setting up your own business, you should spend some time learning about how to become an entrepreneur; and more importantly, why to become an entrepreneur!

There are a host of reasons why you want to consider this path and become an entrepreneur—your own boss! Indeed, entrepreneurship brings with it a lot of uncertainty, but with that level of uncertainty comes tremendous accountability and freedom.

Here you will learn about some interesting reasons why entrepreneurship should be chosen over traditional employment.

Not Every Corporate Environment Deserves Your Creativity

Without a doubt, entrepreneurs are creative people, and it is very common for people like you to feel that you don't fit in, or that your creativity cannot be put to use in that particular environment.

Once the entrepreneur in you comes to life, it can become a little frustrating to embrace and adjust in an environment that does not feel the right place to practice your creativity. Unless and until you take an initiative to become an entrepreneur, you will not be able to discover anything beautiful.

This aspect has been best explained by Steve Jobs when he said, *"When you grow up, you tend to get told that the world is the way it is...Life can be much broader once you discover one simple fact: Everything around you that you call life was made up by people that were no smarter than you. And you can change it, you can influence it...Once you learn that, you will never be the same again."*

You and your creativity are unique. So do not limit your creativity just because there are limitations in the corporate life. Cross that barrier and show your true potential to the world.

You Can Rule Your Life The Way You Want

Finally, you can say goodbye to the boring lifestyle that remains stuck between the 9 and 5. Believe me, the hype around having a flexible lifestyle—something you decide on your own without any boundaries—is worth the hype. However, there's much more to living the lifestyle you want than just freedom. Don't think it is a shortcut because entrepreneurship may demand longer hours of work and much more hard work. It is not a shortcut, just the right path to a better, bigger future and success.

That being said, even though entrepreneurship may require you to put in more effort and hard work, the flexibility that the entrepreneurial lifestyle gives you will be much different than the traditional routine of 9 to 5.

Another perk of having your own lifestyle includes enjoying vacations whenever you want. You are no more bound to have just a two-week paid vacation that the regular corporate life allows.

Entrepreneurship gives you an opportunity to design your

life the way most people can't. It definitely comes with a lot of hard work, leadership skills, the ability to take both risks and responsibility related to work, but it also gives you a chance to shape your life the way you want.

You Can Live Your Passion of Learning and Growing

Entrepreneurs are believed to be natural learners and this is something they should never stop. A number of people relate learning to age, certain achievements, education, or status, but only entrepreneurs believe learning goes on regardless of these factors.

They are keen to learn and grow at every opportunity they get as they are never satisfied with their current level of learning of knowledge—they are always looking for more. If you find this quality in yourself, and believe learning is something that always excites you, and you are never afraid of learning whether it is through formal education or through the discoveries and experiences life brings, then you have definitely found the entrepreneur inside you.

Another major difference between an entrepreneur mindset and a regular mindset is that when entrepreneurs look around, they see only opportunities; whereas when a regular person looks around, all they see are problems. As mentioned earlier, we all have an entrepreneur inside of us, and we just need to make sure we use those skills well.

Entrepreneurs Can Come Up With Unconventional Ideas

With creativity comes an amazing imagination and a bit of insanity too. These are the perfect traits that define an entrepreneur. They have in them everything that can be used to change the world. Just like their ideas do not fit in any corporate environment other than what they build by themselves, similarly they don't adjust to the world around them until they make it according to how they want it to be.

If you find similar ideas in your imagination, you too could become one of those big names. But all you need to do is take your initiative and prove that you have a successful entrepreneur inside of you.

As Albert Einstein puts it, "Logic will get you from A to B. Imagination will take you everywhere." So it's not wrong to be imaginative as long as you are willing to work on it.

Unlimited Possibilities for Making Money

Indeed, that's a huge factor and driving force for entrepreneurs to do what they are best at. Working for a boss at a job, you are actually contributing to his or her wealth; not your own. As far as your earning potential is concerned, it is set by the boss again in a contract agreed upon. In short, your earning possibilities have been affected. Yes, you might get a chance to get a better job opportunity, or grow at the current job in terms of both money and job position, but even those factors are the exception, not the rule.

No matter what you do, how sincere you are, or how long you stay at the job, your earning potential is capped.

On the other hand, setting up your own business and becoming an entrepreneur may not even earn you the same amount as you were getting on your job in the beginning, but those who take the risk and initiative of entrepreneurship are often self-motivated to establish a successful and money-making business.

As mentioned above, it is difficult for entrepreneurs to feel satisfied, and that's nothing different for what their business is capable of. They are not happy with the current activities of the business or the status quo, and continue to grow their business for better status and income.

This further adds to the lifestyle factor—meaning you are the one in control of your destiny. There's no limit to your possibilities of earning depending on how successful your business is, and that's the beauty of entrepreneurship. There are absolutely no gatekeepers to keep your income capped or regulated.

Make Money While You Sleep

Unfortunately, that's not possible if you are working for someone else. You will only be paid for the work you are doing, and for the active hours are you are spending in helping your boss build his or her empire.

A business earns you money even when you are sleeping. It works exactly the same way. Now your team is helping you build that empire. Not only do you enjoy some inactive hours of money making when running a business, but you also tend to enjoy the location independence. No matter where you are in the world, your business will support you and you will not be restricted to move around.

With a business working for you, you can enjoy the freedom to be where you want. This is nothing less than an opportunity because different environments can foster creativity and innovation. So you can sleep or move around and still make money. There's no way you can beat that!

The Opportunity of Building A Lasting Legacy

Once you have your dream business in place and run it successfully, it can be your lasting legacy that can be passed on to your kids and their kids. Something you initiated out of enthusiasm, passion, interest, and probably as a quest for freedom from your 9 to 5 routine, can end up something as big as a successful business that can continue in your family for generations.

While all of this sounds really tempting, and are some of the best reasons for taking up entrepreneurship, it is important to know that entrepreneurship comes with hardships and a lot of dedication. It is not going to be easy, and probably will take much more time until you can call it a lucrative, successful business. Therefore, it is important that you are prepared to take the initiative to turn your dream into a living reality.

Nothing can be achieved until you have a plan in mind. Now that the above mentioned reasons have convinced you to become an entrepreneur, make sure you take each and every step according to your plan.

You will learn about putting a plan and strategies in place for establishing a successful business in the chapters to come.

Questions that First-Time Entrepreneurs Ask

Only once in your life you will get a chance to experience "First-time entrepreneurship." The key to succeed here is that you understand the advantages and disadvantages of being a first-time entrepreneur well. The best way to steer clear of the disadvantages, is to ask questions that every first-time entrepreneur should ask in order to take a more informed initiative.

The following are five of the most important questions that you must ask yourself before officially getting into the business.

1. Is this business idea going to work?

    This requires some serious market research. You must be clear about your idea, and find out if it is compelling enough to engage the audience. How competitively you get into the game plays a major role.

2. What is my current financial standing, and who will provide additional finances if I need them?

    Not every entrepreneur has all the capital he or she needs to set up and run a business. Even small businesses need big capital at times, and it is important for an entrepreneur to have a financial backup plan. To make sure your business does not fail, it is important that you work on your idea and see if you are creating or planning to offer something that is valuable to people. Investors in your business will also focus on your product and the market for your product or service before deciding whether or not to put in their money. Therefore, it is very important that you are aware of who exactly will pay for your business.

3. Why should I only execute *this* idea for my business?

   Because you don't consider it work, but passion. That's something much more than just a moneymaking business for you. You are setting up a system that helps you mold your life the way you want without compromising on anything. You want to enjoy every second you spend at work doing the things you love. That's the biggest and most important reason why only you should execute this idea.

4. What roles will you be delegating to your team members once you are able to expand and grow your business?

   Setting up the roles for your team members as soon as your business gets off the ground is a smart decision. While everyone should have a certain level of authority, they should be aware of where it ends. At the end of the day, the decision-making power should remain with you even though everyone should get a fair chance to contribute their own opinions into it. Valuing your team members is the key to having a team that values your business' goals.

5. Who else is doing it right now? Know about your competition.

    Having as much information as you can gather about your competitors is a must. Having this idea does not really mean it is unique—even though some aspects could be. This will be your strength. Focus on this to make your business stand out amongst the competitors. If you have competitors working on the same idea, it is the strategies you make, and the plan you put into place, that will make your company different from others.

These five questions are some of the important questions that you should start with when starting the journey to entrepreneurship. Getting your answers from the most reliable resources will help you avoid the problems that come with setting up and establishing your business. Do your homework and conduct as much research as possible until you have answers to all the questions mention above.

Chapter 2

Establishing Your Entrepreneur Mindset
Making the Important Shifts

If you have just started identifying the entrepreneur in you, there's a long way to go in order to establish the perfect mindset of an entrepreneur. These shifts are important if you want to operate as a successful entrepreneur. This chapter will highlight the significance of an entrepreneur mindset, and why making that shift is essential for your successful business journey.

Why You Need the Right Entrepreneur Mindset

Being an entrepreneur is not a business model; it's a mindset. If it were up to you, how would you describe an entrepreneur? Optimistic? Dedicated? Passionate?

Indeed, these are some of the most relevant words to describe an entrepreneur, but there is much more to entrepreneurship than only these traits. To establish your own business and build it up, it is important that you think like an entrepreneur. This is why the shift is important.

An entrepreneur does not need an MBA to run a business successfully, but he or she requires a certain mindset that can be cultivated to establish, lead, and grow the business. Business owners who attain this mindset, are the ones who eventually make their business big and successful. There are different aspects associated with the entrepreneur mindset.

You need the right entrepreneur mindset because:

1. **An Entrepreneur Must Anticipate Failure**

    It is very uncommon to find stories where entrepreneurs made it big on their first attempt. Very few people are lucky enough to find a straight path to success. For the rest, this path is loaded with potholes, and the journey is nothing less than a big challenge.

    Regardless of how wonderful your business plan is, every entrepreneur makes mistakes. If you think you will succeed on your first try, go ahead and stop right now. This is much more complicated than you think. Not being able to anticipate failure can be a reason which keeps you from becoming a successful entrepreneur.

Therefore, adopting that mindset is essential.

2. An Entrepreneur Must Learn to Let Go and Delegate

Some of the biggest entrepreneurs and most successful businesses believe in delegating work. They rely on their team members to keep their businesses running effectively and efficiently. Not every entrepreneur can take care of the entire business alone—especially when it starts expanding. Therefore, it is important to appoint a reliable and skilled team of managers who can take the responsibility of the business operations.

As an entrepreneur your role should be to encourage your team of managers to keep up with your vision and ideas, and provide the most suitable tools that help the business grow and succeed. A number of entrepreneurs attribute the success of their company to their ability of letting go and delegating the work to their subordinates.

3. An Entrepreneur Should be Curious

While a certain set of expertise is not a requirement for entrepreneurs, it is generally expected from successful entrepreneurs to have a wide skill set.

They naturally have a curious personality, which never allows them to feel satiated with the amount of knowledge they have. They enjoy learning, and believe in constant evolving. Their thirst for knowledge makes them successful, efficient, and effective. Entrepreneurs make it big by implementing new ideas in the business and learning new skills.

4. **A Successful Entrepreneur Believes in Following their Instincts**

The majority of company founders believe that the ability and willingness of taking risks is what categorizes an individual as a successful entrepreneur. It is the stepping-stone that encourages one to set up a business and run it successfully.

As an entrepreneur, the road to the success of your business is quite rocky where you seem to face different challenges on a daily basis. It is very common for entrepreneurs to find themselves on uncharted territory where there is very little data or research available for making a good decision. That's the point where an entrepreneur must rely on his or her natural instincts and gut feeling. Businesses are risky, but there's a reason that you are an entrepreneur. You should have that ability in you to follow the instincts and take risks.

Some of the most successful entrepreneurs say that sometimes even the smallest lessons and skills can make a big difference to the business.

What Makes You Different?

The Difference between an Entrepreneur Mindset and Employee Mindset

If you are making a transition from being an employee to becoming an entrepreneur, learning about and remembering the difference between the mindset of an employee and an entrepreneur is highly essential.

This topic will cover everything that will help you make that transition. Since you are already planning to become an entrepreneur, there is the possibility that you have already made a silent transition, but to adopt the traits and mindset of a successful entrepreneur, it is important to learn them all.

Believe it or not, being an entrepreneur is all about having the right mindset. It is important to find out whether you have completely transitioned into the mindset of an entrepreneur, or are still somewhat stuck to your employee mindset.

1. **Entrepreneurs Work On Their Skills**

    Unlike entrepreneurs, employees have their focus on their weaknesses more. Instead of identifying and working what they are good at, they keep improving their weaknesses to get better at things.

    "What measures have you taken to overcome that weakness?" is a very sensible and common question for an employee to hear. After all, employees are told what their weaknesses are, and the ways they can improve upon them. This information is irrelevant for entrepreneurs.

Instead of working or improving their weaknesses, they identify and highlight their strength to put it to best use.

2. Entrepreneurs Are Responsible for Decision Making; Both Good and Bad

This comes from the mindset. Entrepreneurs naturally consider it their responsibility to make decisions in the best possible manner to ensure it is in favor of the business. They know how to make the most out of an incredible opportunity to create something big out of totally nothing. This mindset and mental freedom is usually not enjoyed by the employee.

Unless a situation demands a team decision, entrepreneurs can rely on their expertise, experience, judgment of the situation, and natural instincts to make a decision. They do not have to wait for permission or commands to make or implement decisions.

Unlike employees, successful entrepreneurs also understand the sensitivity and time limit for certain opportunities, and consider themselves responsible for the urgency that helps them achieve their goals.

3. Employees Think Before they Start

It is believed that the future growth for employees

is often hindered because they think a lot about perfecting a variety of skills to get on the top. Instead of taking a positive approach before starting anything, they think a lot and create self-doubts on their strengths and capabilities. Entrepreneurs are only aware of what is most important to them. Instead of thinking, they believe in acting. They start their work even if they have very important input. Perfecting skills is more like a time-wasting trap for them. Even though they are constant learners, they believe in learning new things along the journey, but do not delay decisions just because they want to "think" more about it.

After all, business is all about taking risks.

4. Entrepreneurs Consider Learning as a Never-Ending Journey

While there are no restrictions for employees, it is just not in their mindset. Since they are working for other people, they have a specific job description that they have to follow. If they already possess the required skills, they do not focus on learning more.

On the other hand, an entrepreneur involves in constant learning that allows them to keep up with both updated knowledge and newer skills that helps them take the success of their business to the next level. Moreover, constant learning also helps entrepreneurs of small businesses to take care of different aspects of the business due to lack of funds to outsource or hire people for work they don't want to do or are not good at.

This could include setting up a spreadsheet, marketing the business ideas, getting investors for funds, using new and unfamiliar technology for more efficient business operations, or crafting the most suitable pitch for business purposes. However, unlike an entrepreneur, there is no room for excuses for employees. They are hired based on their knowledge and skills; therefore, they need to follow their job description at all costs.

5. **The Freedom of Creativity**

   To a certain extent, you can call this a chance to break rules. This could only be done by an entrepreneur. He or she has the power and ability to enjoy the freedom of creativity, and therefore they can change decisions, plans, and ideas at the last minute if the entrepreneur feels like it. On the other hand, using that same freedom by the employee can be considered as literally breaking the rules and could lead to dismissal.

   On the other hand, entrepreneurs are also not interested in the status quo. They are constantly after opportunities and want to achieve things their way—differently. This also means that entrepreneurs are after acquiring a global perspective to make their freedom of creativity the next big thing their business is remembered for.

What You Need To Do To Shift the Mindset

The following are some things you need to learn to shift the mindset.

1. **Dream Big**

    Entrepreneurs are natural dreamers. As an entrepreneur, you must set your priorities right, and do not hesitate to dream big. Set your goals accordingly. For instance, if you want to double your turnover by the end of the next year, you should take one step at a time, and keep small goals for yourself until you reach your ultimate goal.

    There's nothing wrong with shooting for the stars when setting your own business. However, taking one step at a time, and making your small goals attainable will help you achieve your ultimate goal effortlessly.

    Setting your end goal and keeping your focus on it is essential.

2. **Prep Up for the Challenge**

    Be prepared before facing the real challenge. If you are aware of the situation, customer, product, services, topic, or whatever, you will feel more confident to take up the challenge. With more information in hand, you are totally armed up to provide your point and implement your ideas to take your business to the next level.

This requires that you do one of the following as a successful entrepreneur:

- Practice
- Learn
- Research
- Ask questions
- Read more about the subject
- Listen and keep your information updated

3. Don't Hesitate with Correction while Seeking Inspiration

The right entrepreneurship mindset that leads to success can be achieved by creating the right balance between the delivery method, and the time-tested wisdom that helps you achieve your goal. If you are doing it for the first time, there's no harm in seeking inspiration from those who have already done what you are doing, or who have set examples of things you wish to do or achieve for your business.

This would require some research and homework on your part to find out the best business in your field that you can look up to.

Other than that, it is important that you are receiving information through a method that perfectly works for you. This will allow easy adoption, effective correction and implementation of information once it is received.

4. The Mindset of a Passionate Entrepreneur

Get into a business that you are passionate about. This will help you stick to the plan and stay focused in case you get stuck, or feel defeated at any point. You should have a purpose for getting into a business. What could be better than doing something you are totally passionate about?

Whenever you come around this question, "Is my business really worth it?" or "What else would I do if I didn't own this business?" The answer should satisfy you in every possible manner. When you ask this question, you should never be able to feel like you should give up on your business. You should feel happy, satisfied, and passionate about the work you do. You should also feel confident about the drive you have inside of you for a successful business; passion as well as skills.

While it is important to love what you do, it is also important that you remind yourself on a regular basis the benefits of owning the business and growing it. For majority entrepreneurs, it is the ability that allows the business to establish, flourish, and grow as they continue to do what they love without feeling under pressure or burdened.

5. Seeking Help From External Resources

As an entrepreneur, it is important that you have your mind open to learning and seeking help from external resources. You can start with listening to interviews of successful entrepreneurs, and read books written by or written on the life of successful entrepreneurs. This is indeed a great and effective way to get yourself into the perfect mindset that helps you grow your business and become successful.

Doing so, and gaining knowledge about it, will also help you steer clear of pitfalls other entrepreneurs have experienced. This has worked as an inspiration for various business entrepreneurs. They have followed the same rules and succeeded.

6. **Entrepreneurs Accept and Learn from their Failures**

You need to learn how to embrace failure in order to totally switch to the entrepreneur mindset. It is not easy for first time entrepreneurs to get it right on the first go. Also, it is not easy to accept and learn from failure and continue with the business even if there are defeats.

If you are not able to do so, it means you still need to make that transition. Embracing failure, and learning from those experiences, allows business owners to take a more creative approach to market and sell their products or services. It encourages entrepreneurs to plan and develop more innovative ways to think outside the box, and to take their products or services beyond the competitive landscape for a successful business journey.

With the wrong mindset, dealing with inevitable entrepreneurship fluctuation can be extremely challenging, to say the least. It is very important to shift the mindset to what successful entrepreneurs have.

Entrepreneurial Development Levels

Just like not all business owners are true entrepreneurs, not all entrepreneurs are equal. Just like any other skill, entrepreneurship has different development levels that help an individual business owner to evolve and become an effective entrepreneur.

The five different entrepreneurial levels and their mindsets are discussed below. These entrepreneurial levels revolve around the belief systems, thinking patterns, and entrepreneurial mindsets of different entrepreneurs at different entrepreneurial development levels.

Let's find out more about each of these levels in detail.

The Self-Employed Mindset

The driving force behind entrepreneurs at the first level of entrepreneurial development level is much more than finding security on a personal level. These individuals are after achieving greater control over their lives, destiny, financial gains, and overall career.

These people are not happy with their 9 to 5 routine, or receiving orders from their bosses. Their idea of happiness is beyond that boundary that makes them believe that their job would be much more efficient and lucrative without an employer—and possibly even without the need of employees to a certain extent.

The entrepreneurs with the self-employed mindset desire more independence. The do not want interference from any one when they are doing things their way. And often, they start with establishing a business that they are truly interested in or passionate about so they do not need help from external resources to establish it.

Unfortunately, this does not work for everyone, and very few people do great here and evolve toward the next level. The primary objective of achieving freedom to becoming an entrepreneur only for the sake of self-employment and control mindset end up in traps and pitfalls. This usually happens because they want to remain a sole entity establishing and running the business.

By totally shutting people out—even employees and team members in some cases—sometimes entrepreneurs deprive themselves of intelligence, valuable talent, experience, and feedback that other individuals can offer by becoming a part of the team.

There are a number of entrepreneurs who switch to entrepreneurship with the do-it-yourself mindset. They may achieve self-satisfaction and happiness by becoming their own boss, but may fail at establishing a profitable company or a new career.

While entrepreneurs are looking for freedom, individuals at the first level often have to spend more time and hard work in establishing and running the business. While they are not working for anyone else, their job becomes much more consuming. They may enjoy no holidays, might even have to bring loads of work home with them, and might even have to spend more hours working just to up their financial compensation. Their motto, "Do everything yourself when you can, without delegating the job to anyone else," can actually cost them more than benefitting them. Sometimes they don't even have a team to work with, and as a result, they become the sole responsible for business operations. Clients look up to them and bring their feedback—both negative and positive—to deal directly with the entrepreneur. As a result, the entrepreneur feels burned out completely.

One of the biggest drawbacks of this entrepreneurship level is that self-employed entrepreneurs try to get into the same business as they were hired in before to utilize the level of experience and expertise from what they have already learnt. This restricts them from exploring their strengths, interest, and passion.

For entrepreneurs on the first level, it is very important to know the importance of designing a business pattern that works for them, instead of the entrepreneur working all day long all alone. This step is essential for becoming a true entrepreneur, and for running a successful venture. Entrepreneurs who can easily understand this, and are ready to interpret this, can rise to the second level of entrepreneurship discussed below.

Building The Managerial Perspective

Entrepreneurs on the second level have a natural managerial outlook toward setting up their own business, and are definitely at a much better place to flourish as successful entrepreneurs. However, at level two, two major misconceptions can lead to a lot of trouble.

First, entrepreneurs with a managerial perspective may tend to believe that if a business is constantly failing to grow, the solution could be in hiring more employees to take responsibility for the business. Throwing extra people to resolve the problem mostly ends up in aggravating the situation because the underlying root cause of that leads to failure is still not addressed. Hiring more people may not help entrepreneurs find the real problem that is causing them trouble.

Secondly, these entrepreneurs also tend to believe that the only way they can achieve success is through growth; not profit growth, but growth in the overall structure of the business. Having the managerial perspective toward running a business, these entrepreneurs tend to rely more on human resources, and tend to believe the bigger the team, the better. Unfortunately, businesses today run on a completely different level to grow both internally and externally.

On the other hand, experts believe that growing larger is not a solution if you really want to address and fix the problem. In fact, the larger the business gets, one can only expect the problems to magnify. Many entrepreneurs with managerial perspectives end up in bankruptcy because of their focus in vigorous growth in the size of the company without really addressing the problem at the root.

While the above mentioned two are the major misconceptions that could lead to problems for managerial entrepreneurs, there are other aspects of their attitude that could damage the company. Since the perspective is managerial, the entrepreneur wants to be the "Boss." While this is important to a certain aspect, sometimes managerial entrepreneurs do it at the sake of the potential talent of their employees. They like to take the lead, but not to show or draw the path, but to become in-charge and give orders, which does not require great aptitude or skill. Their approach should be to become a leader; one who is not only skilled, but who knows how to train and inspire others to follow the right path for bigger success.

In order to work successfully at this level and with the mindset of a managerial entrepreneur, it is important that they learn how to become leaders and get the most out of their managers and employees. They should focus on setting higher goals and addressing problems at the root using minimal human resource to resolve the issue quickly and much more efficiently. Entrepreneurs who work to gain the level of "Leader" experience remarkable benefits as far as the success of their business is concerned.

Therefore, it is extremely important to make use of your managerial skills in the right way and use your human resources in the most efficient manner.

The Right Attitude of A Leader

Attaining the third level of entrepreneurship in itself is a big deal. If you have reached this level, it is a sign that you might enjoy remarkable benefits as an entrepreneur if you know how to operate the business without constantly looking after it, and by letting your employees do work on your behalf, as it operates and earns you profits without your 100% participation.

This sort of entrepreneurship, with the positive and right approach, can set up an organization that is more self-sustaining and self-sufficient and grows in term of more wealth as well as the structure. Moreover, setting up a business like that helps the entrepreneur enjoy what he or she has been aiming for—

more free time, more personal freedom, and most importantly, more money.

In short, it is more like making money while you are asleep or having fun at some exotic destination with your loved ones while your business continues to earn you wealth.

Instead of taking all the work on your own as a sole entity, believing that you can still get the job done in the most efficient manner is the way to go. Being an entrepreneur, you act as a leader who has passed the torch of both expertise and responsibilities to your team members who continue to work on your business in order to achieve your aim for their own career achievements.

This brings you to a position where your focus should only be on the net earnings of the business, instead of keeping track of the revenues and sales. While the control stays in your hand, the operations are in the hands of the more skilled people who are working under your supervision to build more wealth and grow your business for you. While the business continues to operate smoothly and earns you more money, you, as an entrepreneur, can concentrate on the control aspects and fine-tuning of your business for smoother operations and increased profitability.

Mindset of an Entrepreneurial Investor

This is a level where you are mentally prepared for bigger challenges as an entrepreneur. Since you have already achieved a steady running business that is generating profits without your constant hands-on participation, it is time to take one step forward and prepare yourself for bigger, yet exciting challenges, which is money management to produce more money.

Yes, we are talking about smart investments here. Now that you have your pockets full of money that your business is generating for you, put your focus on using that money to produce some more. Investing in order to maximum returns does not only require skills, but smart leverage of assets and assessments. A smart and successful entrepreneur will leverage the success of his or her initially organized business to create another business—or businesses—following the same profitable and success system or model.

The investor can evolve the existing business by buying other businesses or franchising the successful ventures through investments. This allows the entrepreneurial investor to sell basic services and products along with the entire business. The ultimate goal of the entrepreneur, however, will still be to earn bigger profits.

This is the point where a smart entrepreneurial investor will look for businesses—for either refurbishing or buying—to run it in the same way that earns them bigger profits. Using the money you are generating from your first business to invest in other profitable businesses, requires comprehensive strategies. Moreover, working smartly can also replace working hard; whereas the rewards can be much more than what you have been earning with working hard.

Aspects of a True Entrepreneurial Mindset

As you move from level one all the way to level five, you will learn various new things, and continue to evolve learning the different sides of entrepreneurship. This will help you achieve the insights for your entrepreneurial accomplishment, where you can easily achieve your ultimate goal, and realize you are literally one step away from that life-changing experience for which you took entrepreneurship.

This is the final step and here you will experience that an entrepreneur goes through a paradigm shift that includes a different thinking process based on four essential steps:

- **Idealization:** Upgrading your mindset to imagine all-encompassing, gigantic dreams that you once thought were impossible to achieve. Imagining what you want to achieve can create the ideal world around you.

- **Visualization:** Use your imagination for visualization. Picture that ideal world you want to achieve, and start with clarifying this vision taking one step at a time. Add more details to your ultimate goal with each passing day to bring more visualization to your imagination.

- **Verbalization:** Your visualization can now be put into words, and you may talk about it as if it really is going to happen. Talk to others about it and continue as if it was real. Talk to your team so they can see your vision clearly too.

- **Materialization:** Since the intention and effort of believing and designing the ideal world is now being talked about, you will see how things would automatically start falling into place in the most natural way. What you once imagined is not an idea anymore. It is a tangible fact that you can definitely give a shape. As an entrepreneur, it will open new doors to fresh opportunities for the growth and success of your business.

An entrepreneur only dreams, but a true entrepreneur ensures the dreams come true. Focusing on these aspects, learning from the mistakes, and continuing to evolve as an entrepreneur until you reach the fifth and final stage, is the best way to enjoy running your own profitable venture.

By examining these essential phases of entrepreneurship, you can gain a better understanding of aspects that could help you easily distinguish between the ordinary and extraordinary entrepreneurs. And you don't want to settle for the least. So make sure you continue to evolve and grow!

Chapter 3

Write the Vision
Setting Your Goal the Right Way

Goals help entrepreneurs set the right direction for the business so that they can be achieved and the business can be called successful. Without setting goals, a business has no definite purpose, and no aspiration to strive for. As a consequence, businesses struggle for meaningful accomplishments and eventually fail.

Goals are essential for a business as they are stepping stones that take us closer to achievement of bigger ambitions. In short, every business that wants to be successful should have a goal, as well as a business plan, that helps the entrepreneur and the team to achieve that goal.

Setting up your business means your first step should be to come up with a goal right away.

Setting Up a Business
Importance of Setting Goals to Achieve

But why is that the first step, and why is it that important? Writing your vision down for your successful business as an entrepreneur is important and there are several reasons for that.

Before we go ahead and find out why it is important to set goals as your first step to setting up a business, let us first look into the definition of goals for entrepreneurs.

What Are Goals?

These are resolutions that take us closer to success as we reach our desired result. Goals are both short-term and long-term, and have different purposes. But regardless of the term of the goal, they are set to provide a clear understanding to both the entrepreneur and their team of what the business is striving to achieve.

Setting short-term goals is key to achieve long-term goals. This is more like taking one step at a time to get closer to your ultimate goals, and thus, is the foundation to a successful business. As an entrepreneur, setting goals as your first step to setting up a business is also important as it helps you design the plan too. Starting without any scope is a hopeless attempt that is never successful. However, if you have a goal and a plan in hand to achieve that goal, there is much more hope for the business to become successful in no time. Having your goals set gives everyday tasks and operations carried out in the business more meaning, and even clarifies the reasoning behind decisions that are taken within the company.

Why Should We Set Goals For Our Business

As a successful entrepreneur, it is your responsibility to set goals for your business if you want to see it grow and become successful. You do not necessarily have to do this alone. If you are working with a team, it is ideal if you have a discussion with them before setting the ultimate goals for your business. In case you are starting as a sole entity to set up your business, feel free to discuss and take advice from people in your family and social circle who have an experience with this.

The following are some of the most important reasons why setting goals is necessary.

1. **Measuring Success**

   Unless you have your end goal set, you won't be able to measure if you are improving, growing and moving toward achieving your ultimate goal. While your goal could be different, the most common goal for a majority of businesses is to become more profitable and powerful in terms of money and status.

   When you have the goals in place, it will provide you the clearest way to measure the success of your business as you continue to evolve. When you foresee the future of your business for the next three or five years, you should be able to look beyond the tactical side of the business, and keep your approach much more narrow.

This will allow you to judge your business and its success from a business economic and competitive perspective.

2. **Leadership Assessment**

    As an entrepreneur, you will be operating like a leader that the team members will look up to. When you have your goals in place, your next step should be to ensure that your team members are all willing to help you achieve that goal. Therefore, you must ensure that your team members are aware of the prize and the ultimate goal.

    It is important that their personal/career achievements are associated with the achievements of the business to keep up with their interests. Moreover, when your team clearly understands the ultimate goal of your business, it provides a greater rationale for the decisions you, as an entrepreneur, might have to make with respect to acquisitions, hiring, sales programs, incentives, and other financially driven decisions.

    This will allow you to waive off a great amount of uncertainty, and your team will be highly motivated to achieve the goal of your company for you.

3. **Gaining Knowledge is Essential**

    With the goals already set and defined, you, as

an entrepreneur, can develop a better understanding of your decision-making. It also shows you how your decision-making will affect your journey toward your ultimate goal.

For instance, when you are working with a budget that clearly defines your spending power against the revenue earned, you can easily understand the implications of a certain decision, and if it is really worth it to make the decision at a cost or not.

As an entrepreneur, you must believe that knowledge is power, and the more information you have, the more you are in control of your business and your decision-making.

4. **Reassessing If You Are Heading in the Right Direction**

Monitoring the success of your business on the goals you have set initially will also help you determine if you made the right choice. Monitoring the growth and performance of your business against the goals will help you decide whether you want to continue with the same goals, or change midway for better outcomes.

If you find out that your financial projections and other aspects of decision-making were wrong while you established your initial goals, you can reassess the growth midway, and modify your goals and plans accordingly. This way, it is also easy to target the weaknesses and adjust accordingly.

It is highly important to remember that setting goals while you are establishing your business does not guarantee success for your business. While it is an important aspect, the way your business operations are carried out, or the motivation level of your employees, can create a big difference to your bottom-line. While we cannot predict the future, ensuring that the operations are effective, and the employees are also actively working toward achieving the goal, and assessing the plan and goals midway are some successful ways you can optimize setting goals.

Plan for it, but do not rely on it completely.

Why You Should Only Set "SMART" Goals

Nothing could be worse than realizing that your goals are no longer working in your favor. It could be rather disappointing to find out that both the goals and plan should be changed since the midway assessment of the goals showed weak results.

As mentioned earlier, we cannot really predict the future. But we sure can plan one and work accordingly to ensure we achieve it. This is where SMART goals come in. If you do your research and set a SMART goal right in the beginning when you are setting up your business, you will not have to change route midway.

SMART is an acronym for five elements which are:

S = Specific

M = Measurable

A = Attainable

R = Relevant

T = Timely

These are the five elements that your goal should be based on. It is a very simple tool used by businesses for a very long time to set their goals, and helps the entrepreneur to go beyond the regular goal-setting process in order to set up a goal that offers desirable results in the end.

The Goal Should Be "Specific"

Goals that end up in positive and desirable results are focused and well-defined. The more specific you are about your goal, the more of your focus you can put in. It makes your goal become more attractive, which naturally pulls you in, along with the resources for efficient usage.

Similarly, being specific allows your energies to become more focused too, and that's where you are in the power of generating more and more until you achieve your desirable results. A goal that is specific has a greater chance of being accomplished. Questions like who, what, when, where, and why, will help you make your approach as specific as possible.

The Goal Should Be "Measurable"

Setting a goal that does not have a measurable result is like giving an examination without any examiner or grading system; totally pointless.

Since the goal is being set for your business, having your numbers calculated and in place is important. These are an essential part of running a successful business. Put in specific and concrete numbers while setting your goals to keep track of your performance as an entrepreneur, as well as the performance of your team carrying out the real operations.

Measuring your progress will not only help you stay on track, but will also help you hit your targets in a timelier manner. Questions like how many, or how much, or how will I know if I have accomplish… will help you set more measurable goals.

The Goal Should Be "Attainable"

Sure, you can think about a goal of setting up your own big-scale restaurant. However, in order to achieve that goal, you will need a huge capital, the right location, investors, and a detailed analysis of the expenses. The resources required, or the plan you need to put in place to set your goal, is what makes it attainable. However, if you lack the resources, or if the plan sounds too good to be true, then the goal is not attainable.

It is a very important aspect of setting goals, and if the plans and resources do not seem reasonable, the goal cannot be achieved.

The Goal Should Be "Relevant"

Achieving the goals you have set for your business is based on the realities and current conditions the business is operating in. Therefore, it is essential that your goal should smartly fit into your business model. When setting up a business, every entrepreneur first designs a business plan. It is important to refer to this plan while setting your goals. This will keep you more realistic and relevant. Don't try to pull everything at once. Focus on what is more relevant and easily achievable.

Working on your business plan and improving your goal relevance in respect to both client and customer engagement and the overall business climate will keep you on point.

The Goal Should Be "Timely"

Is there a right time to work on your business objectives? Indeed!

You must know when you should bring your business into operation to achieve the goals you have set. You should also be aware of how much time each phase requires once your business has been set up. You should consider constructing a working calendar to know you are managing everything timely.

Business objectives without any deadlines or time limits can become too vague. They are absolutely useless because you have not set a certain time limit to achieve them. Therefore, it is highly important to keep up with time management for your business. This will also help you keep a track of all the other factors of setting up a smart goal mentioned above.

In case a phase is taking too long and does not even guarantee great outcomes, it may not work. So put your brain to work and consider all of these important aspects.

Setting "SMART" Goals

In addition to being a catchy acronym, SMART means much more when it comes to setting your business goals. It is more of a strategy that's well-considered, fixable, quantifiable, and flexible. While considering all of the above mentioned factors, it is important to rely on your market research, knowledge, and even guts, to run your business successfully as an entrepreneur. There are times when a goal might look feasible keeping the SMART aspects in mind, but you might have to make a decision against it because the market is not acceptable of such goals, or if there is a sudden shift in trend in the market. Therefore, all these factors matter and should be taken into account.

As a small business, you might set up your business goal all on your own or after taking input from your team members. As a business that wants to evolve and grow on a continuous basis, make sure you have both short-term and long term goals in place. Both of them are essential for measuring success. That's also the most effective way to add value to your business.

So set **SMART** goals so that you keep pushing your business toward its ultimate success.

What Are Vision Boards and How to Use Them for Goal Setting

We have a business culture that does not consider organizations and entrepreneurs successful until they have achieved their goals. And the best ways entrepreneurs use to keep themselves motivated to achieve these goals is the continuous strive to achieve bigger and better, improvement, and dedication. They do not hesitate in working harder and increasing productivity for desirable outcomes.

Setting business goals is just like setting a New Year's Resolution. You have a goal in mind, but it is so broad and unspecified that it cannot be achieved. "I will lose weight," "I will follow a healthy lifestyle," "I will make more money," are some of the most common goals people have in their mind at the start of each year. But you never actually get there because you have not yet figured out how to achieve that goal.

All of these are also true for setting goals for your business. While every business wants to earn more money, become more successful, and grow rapidly, there is no plan in place that could be followed to achieve these goals.

Now that you have learned a few interesting goal setting factors, it is time to implement them. Here's another amazing method that will help you with business goal setting without any trouble.

Think about getting a vision board in place for your goal setting this year. If for all of your life, you thought vision boards were a bogus, you have been missing out on a lot.

Having your own board that displays where you want to see your business in the next couple of years, or a board that displays the path to ultimate success, can actually help you achieve it effortlessly. It is common for us to expand on whatever we focus on. When you have a vision board displaying everything you want to achieve for your business, you essentially end up visualizing it, which further motivates you and keeps you on track.

It is very important that this vision board is placed somewhere where you see it multiple times during the day. Since it is related to your business and is a great motivating factor not only for you, but your team members, it is ideal to adjust it within your workplace so that your team members can also see it on a daily basis, and can refresh in their head what they are looking forward to achieving.

Doing so naturally puts you in a state where you observe short visualization exercises during the day.

Believe it or not, visualization is an extremely powerful exercise that you can practice. It works, especially if you believe in it. But considering it magic is also not the right approach. Just pasting things and drafting a plan for your goal on a cardboard will not give you results. It is the visualization and the impact of seeing your goals on a daily basis that reminds you to stay dedicated and focused, and moving toward achieving your goal.

If you are working with a team, you may want to consider creating a vision board that displays goals for everyone to keep them motivated. For instance, if the growth of the company in terms of bigger profits and bigger team size is your goal for the business, it should also display how moving toward this goal will benefit the team members on an individual level—the vision board should show the personal growth they can achieve if the company grows. Since everyone would be able to see their specific goals on the vision board, it will keep them focused and motivated to push themselves further.

If you have never created a vision board before, the process is pretty simple. The following are the things you will need to put everything in place:

- Scissors
- A large poster board (you can go as large as you want to, keeping in mind that it can be placed in your office)
- Glue
- Pictures of you and your team members that you can cut and paste along with different goals
- Tape (regular or double-sided)
- Inspirational business magazines for the cutouts
- Pictures or logos that display how you want to grow your business.
- Additional stickers and pointers for further detailing

Your options are literally limitless, keeping in mind your business and respective goals. Take help from your team members, and put the board up in the most creative and inspirational way possible so it catches your eye whenever you pass by it.

Once the board is complete, look at it and see if it is instantly tweaking your brain and pushing you toward the goal and keeping you focused. Adjust it if it needs more improvement. Moreover, go ahead and continue to make changes as you keep hitting your short-term goals. Don't forget to celebrate your little victories and share them with your team members to keep them motivated until your bigger and ultimate goals are hit.

You might want to create annual vision boards with different and more improved goals for each year. While this requires both time and creativity, it is going to be so worth it if you put it to use!

A Goal-Supporting System
Creating the Right System to Achieve Your Goals

As an entrepreneur, you are responsible to put a goal supporting system in place that takes you closer to achieving your goals and making your business a big success. As an entrepreneur, it is also important to understand that implementing and achieving goals can be highly overwhelming if a proper system is not put in place beforehand.

An effective system is important to help you track your pace as well as monitor the progress you are making toward achieving your goals.

Setting Realistic, Achievable Goals

First of all, you need to assess the current system that is already in place. When you are re-setting your goal, it is important that you find out what you have been missing out in the system previously. For instance, if you have set your goal to achieve bigger profits by hiring more employees, which has never worked out in your favor before, setting the same goal again, without changing the path, is like moving toward failure again.

If you are working on the budget of your business and trying to cut down on expenses for bigger profits, it is important that you set up a support system that allows better utilization of resources. If you aim for bigger profits, without examining your current expenses and the ways to control them, the result would also be a failed attempt. Therefore, it is essential to set up an effective system in place with realistic expectations that you know you can achieve.

Keep the Right Approach

Start with finding the glitch in your current system so that you know about the areas that need some work. You can come up with a plan and implement a system that actually works.

Work With Your Team

Find a team that becomes your support system for achieving your financial goals. Working with a team brings out your human resources and creativity of multiple people together. With the right decisions, you can put the most effective and efficient team to work to achieve your business goal for you.

As you go on to set more and more goals for your business, you might have to put different systems in place for everything to work according to the plan. Moreover, as an entrepreneur, it is important that you keep things organized so that the operations can be carried out smoothly.

Look for a path that works for you, and don't forget to be creative with your approach.

Five Important Goals You Should Not Miss Out On as an Entrepreneur

Entrepreneurs live with big dreams and lofty goals. They aim for higher leads, bigger paychecks, and more sales. So what's wrong with that? Nothing! These are definitely some of the best goals to have as an entrepreneur. The problem occurs when these entrepreneurs try to bypass all the short-term goals for the sake of achieving long-term goals.

While every business has its own set of goals to achieve, there are certain goals that all entrepreneurs should take into account. Instead of setting objectives that are far-fetched, setting goals that are more reasonable will help you take your business to the next level without a lot of effort.

So what are some reasonable goals you should set as an entrepreneur after determining all of your goals are SMART? The following is a list of five important goals:

Boost Sales

The best way to earn more money is to boost sales and control expenses. This would increase the revenue for the business, and will also offer a reasonable growth rate that would help you expand your business with time. However, boosting sales does not really mean setting unrealistic goals.

While rapid growth rate sounds very attractive, it does not always work that way, and eventually you might feel demotivated with time. Working slowly and steadily toward boosting your sales will help you grow your business. It takes a small business time to be fully prepared to transform on a large scale. Therefore, growing too much and too quickly can lead to mishandling.

Slow and steady wins the race! Make sure you focus on growth even if it is only a small one.

Achieving an Active Online Space

Set up your website if it is already not there. If you already have a website, make sure you re-design or update it as often as possible to keep it effective and interactive. This is one aspect often overlooked since the entrepreneur and other team members are busy with other business operations.

If you have been doing the same, know that you have been missing out on a huge market. The world has gone online today and not giving time to your online presence can affect the operation of your business.

Make sure you dedicate some time to your online presence and give it an interactive makeover.

Increasing Human Resources

Your next most important goal should be to increase your team size. This will eventually have an impact on the growth of your business too. However, this decision could be a little overwhelming, especially if you are running a small business or have been a one-man show throughout.

If you have not hired a team yet—and have only been

working with virtual assistant or freelancers—you might want to consider having one team member to start with. Hiring a whole team could be difficult to manage in the beginning, and therefore starting with an individual working for you on a full-time basis should be your ultimate goal.

This process is time consuming, and it is highly advised that you take your time to ensure you are working with the right people. At the same time, it is also important that you utilize the human resources in the best possible manner for the success of your business.

Expand Your Business Operations

Whether it is about increasing your product line or the services you offer, as an entrepreneur, your goal should be to expand your business operations.

For instance, you have only been providing services so far, introducing your first product is also considered as an expansion and vice versa. Whenever you feel you are ready to productize your business, go ahead and let your business make some passive income.

Cut Costs for Bigger Profits

Since your ultimate goal is to earn more money, you should find different ways to achieve that goal as an entrepreneur. Reducing expenses by cutting cost within your business operations is a great and realistic way to achieve that goal. Find out areas where the cost can be cut down, and utilize resources in the most efficient way possible for best results.

Reasonable Goals are Best Goals

As an entrepreneur, you are very well aware that setting up and operating your business is not easy. Therefore, it is highly important that you keep your goals reasonable so that you set yourself up for success and not failure. Keeping your goals reasonable and SMART is the key.

Chapter 4

Taking Care of Essential Entrepreneurial Aspects: Time Management

Whether you assign time a dollar value or not, there is no doubt how valuable it is for us—and especially for entrepreneurs. Imagine how much time you spend under stress of not being able to complete your work or achieve your goal just because you do not have enough time. Since you are an entrepreneur, time management is highly important for you if you want to run your business successfully.

Today, there are a number of ways to manage time issue—organizers, listing, adjusting your sleep time and work routine, maintaining it through the app, etc. But before we move onto that, it is important to learn why time management is a critical aspect of entrepreneurship.

Why Time Management is Critical for Entrepreneurs

If you focus on the big picture, you will know why time management for entrepreneurs is critical. It is very important for an entrepreneur to manage their time effectively in order to gain all the benefits it has to offer. Here are some important reasons why time management is crucial.

Because Time is Limited

Regardless of how you chop it down, you have only 24 hours to spend in a day. This is applicable on you, as well as on all of your team members who only seem to work half the time you do. However, the same time is also allowed to other team members of yours who are consistently working much more than you do, and who are accomplishing more for your business.

This is because one individual is utilizing that time in a much efficient manner than the other one—and probably even better than you. In short, you just need to acknowledge and learn the importance of using these limited resources in an extremely efficient manner to make the most out of it. Since time is limited, rising through it will raise your rank.

There are Great Learning Opportunities

This is applicable for you as well as your employees. Time gives you opportunities and allows you to learn more and make the most out of those opportunities. All you need is some time to dedicate to these opportunities and take advantage of them.

At the same time, you should allow your employees to do the same by offering these opportunities to them so that they learn and implement.

Benefits You Can Guarantee with Time Management

Time management is an important aspect of entrepreneurship. It helps proper utilization of resources keeping in mind your end goal. It is also essential because it offers you bigger benefits for your business than you think.

Interestingly, the benefits of time management will vary greatly for us since our businesses, business plans, and goals, are different from each other. However, there are some universal benefits that you can achieve as entrepreneurs. These are listed below.

- Since you know time is a scarce resource, you put better focus so that you achieve your goal in lesser time.
- Managing time efficiently helps you make more money.
- By utilizing time in the most effective manner, you can enjoy more free time at hand, and can spend it doing things you like or with friends and family.
- Time management helps you schedule your own lifestyle the way you want it without compromising on your business.
- You have more time in hand for pursuing hobbies, passions, and travel.
- Gives you peace of mind because you are utilizing this scarce resource in the most efficient manner and will already be ahead

of your timetable.

Other than personal use of the spare time you have in hand, you can utilize the spare time for the benefits of your business. For instance, if you are making the most of time management and accomplishing a target in a week's time that you used to take a month for previously, you have three additional weeks in hand that you can invest in the business for better operations, strategy building, and planning.

It is all about how you plan to use the time.

Setting the Right Time Management Plan for Your Business

As an entrepreneur, you are responsible to fulfill a leadership role in your organization. As a result, your time does not only belong to you, but your team members too.

Even if you try hard, you can always expect to experience unlimited interruptions, time-bending encounters, and requests from your team members throughout the day. This could easily take you off of your scheduled time table or the time management policy you have been following.

At work, your ability to keep up with effective time management will have a positive overall impact on your business. The following are four important factors that you should consider in order to set the right time management plan for your business.

Make the Most Out of Technology

Use technology—all of it! The efficiency technology brings can ease out lives and business operations. In fact, today technology has evolved to a point that it can even act as a personal assistant and can replace human resources in various areas—especially in businesses based on manufacturing of products.

Successful entrepreneurs around the world rely on technology to keep up with their time and tasks. Using technology can effectively help you with time management. And you do not have to get yourself custom-made machineries for that. Just having your tablet, smartphone, or laptop can keep you right on the schedule as it can alert you for scheduled events and upcoming meetings without failing.

There are various apps designed to help you as an entrepreneur. Some will help you maintain lists and reminders, while others would allow you to set alarms for important dates, and store voice memos and notes. While you might have to pay for some of these apps, others are available for free and do not give you an excuse for not utilizing technology and tools for boosting time management for benefiting your business.

Review Your Schedule before Beginning the Day

Reviewing your entire schedule at the start of the day can save you a lot of time and make you more productive. It is important to take some time to review and plan for the activities you will be carrying out during the day. Since you know your schedule best, only you can decide how you want to plan things in the most effective way.

So take your time and plan before starting the day. It also gives you an opportunity to identify potential problems with the schedule and re-plan things to save more and more time. Just spending five minutes in the morning to review your day's schedule increases your likelihood of spending a productive day without wasting time!

Prioritize—
What's the Difference between Important and Urgent

Prioritizing solves more than half of your time management problems. As an entrepreneur, you are expected to survive in an environment with constant interruptions. Your team members can easily and directly access you to address some important and urgent things that you might have to adjust in your schedule without prior notice.

Learning to deal with this distraction through successful time management skills makes you a great entrepreneur. However, to achieve this, it is very important that you focus more on planning and fixing your schedule.

This is why it is crucial to understand the different between urgent and important tasks. It is advised that you should give your priority to events and tasks that are critical (important) and not just urgent. For instance, answering your phone call while you were replying to your emails as per your schedule, is an exception anyone would make. Therefore, make your decisions wisely.

It is also important to remember that this tip applies to both technological as well as human interruptions. You have to immediately carry out this mental calculation to find out if the task is more urgent than critical, or if it can be delayed to complete the more important tasks first.

Do not rely on tools completely for better time management and to regain your time. Prioritize and use this most scarce resource with responsibility for best results.

The following are some interesting time management strategies that you can implement in your business for smoother and successful entrepreneurship.

- Create a to-do list on a daily, weekly, and/or monthly, basis to keep your schedule more organized.
- Once the list has been created, prioritize on the basis of what's critical and what's urgent.
- Give 100% to utilize the resource of time when you are at work.
- Emails could be stealing your time—manage your emails.
- Identify time thieves and take measures to prevent them right away.
- Change lifestyle habits that could be eating your time or making you waste this scarce resource.
- Avoid private use of your cell phone at work.
- Learn to say "no" to make the most out of your time.

Chapter 5

Understanding Core Leadership

A successful entrepreneur is also a leader, but assuming that all entrepreneurs are leaders is wrong. In fact, leadership skills are what make an entrepreneur successful. However, people often confuse core leadership and entrepreneurship and think these are the same terms.

If you have been following that myth too, it is time to learn facts about these two terms and what they mean.

What is Leadership and how is it Different from Entrepreneurship?

"True entrepreneurs are driven to serve as much as they are called to lead." ~Jonathan Fields

"What's the difference between entrepreneurship and leadership" is a common question that could pop up in your mind, especially if you think all entrepreneurs are leaders.

What is Leadership?

Wikipedia describes leadership as, *"The process of social influence in which one person can enlist the aid and support of others in the accomplishment of a common task."* Leadership can be effectively practiced when you also have the ability to utilize and integrate available resources in the most effective way in both internal and external environments of the business.

The most important characteristic of a leader is his or her ability to "socially influence" people around them. While anyone can become a boss and get their commands fulfilled, very few possess this quality of becoming a "social influence" through his or her own acts and exemplification. For an entrepreneur to be successful, it is important that he or she adopts important leadership skills and become the leader that people would love to follow.

On the other hand, we all know what an entrepreneurship is. While a leader may not necessarily be an entrepreneur, an entrepreneur must be a leader in order to run his or her business successfully. They should recognize the importance of delivering highest value to their team members, as well as their organization and should have the ability to execute on that pattern.

Adopting the Most Important Leadership Qualities to Become a Successful Entrepreneur

While the two terms are different, there are common factors between leadership and entrepreneurship. For instance, both leaders and entrepreneurs are imitative-takers. They do not hesitate in raising their hand when a challenge comes up and they take pride in taking risks.

While some leaders are born, others can be made if they learn the leadership skills. If you are an entrepreneur born with leadership qualities, you have everything it takes to become a successful entrepreneur if you utilize the knowledge and available resources in the most effective manner. However, if you think you lack those leadership qualities and are thinking of delegating the leadership task to one of your senior team members, know that skills can be learned.

The following are the five most important, core qualities of leadership that can be learned to experience entrepreneurial leadership effectively.

Vision

Leaders have a vision of seeing things that haven't occurred yet. To be an entrepreneurial leader, it is important that you adopt that vision to foresee the future problems as well as the opportunities to take measures accordingly.

In order to be an entrepreneurial leader, you must utilize your brainpower and imagination to see the outcome of your decisions made today, keeping in mind all the important factors associated with it. Your vision should allow you to access unforeseen information in precise detail so you can save your business from uninformed problems. On the other hand, this ability will also help you see bigger opportunities so you can make the most out of it.

Commitment

Leaders are committed. This quality is also common in entrepreneurs because commitment and dedication to work is the key that drives them toward their goal. However, entrepreneurial leadership requires commitment that encourages you to modify your strategies to adjust with unforeseen circumstances.

It gives them the courage to move forward, keeping up with the commitment, despite the setbacks, unfortunate circumstances, and obstacles.

It is a very important leadership quality that helps them keep going despite the hardships when everyone else wants to give up. This quality is very important for the success of your business. As mentioned earlier, setting up your own business is going to be a challenge, and there will be many instances when you will feel it is not going to work.

That's where this leadership commitment will help you keep going until you achieve your goal.

Strategy and Planning

Leaders are strategy builders and planners. Not all entrepreneurs have these skills—especially those working with team. They often tend to delegate the task of strategy building and planning to the team members too. However, a great entrepreneurial leader is one who can set the strategy, and plan to achieve the business goal all by him or herself.

Your first task would be to set your goal and then create plans and strategies to bridge the distance between your current business aim and your business goal.

As an entrepreneurial leader, you are expected to come up with a step-by-step master plan that helps bridge the difference. Once the plan is in place, the job of your team members will be to follow that plan, utilize the resources efficiently, and make sure the goal is achieved.

Don't forget to set the deadlines to make this more challenging and interesting.

Discernment

As an entrepreneurial leader, you are expected to make important decisions that naturally fall in line with the overall strategy or business plan you have in mind. There will be situations when you have to make an important decision without any prior notice. You had no calculations done on your part, and the decision has to be made urgently.

Discernment is a great leadership quality that will bring out the ability in you to make these unexpected, in-time decisions that do not contradict with your overall plan and strategies or your goals.

It is all about learning and understanding what actions serve your overall interest—keeping your team in mind.

Communication

Different types of leaders have different ways to communicate their business strategies, plans and ideas. The only thing you need to pay attention to is finding the right mode and style of communication that works in your favor. You do not have to necessarily follow an inspiration here. Just try out the different styles and see which one is most suitable for your entrepreneurial leadership.

Your aim should be to get the word out through the most influential way possible so that your team remains motivated, and constantly works to take you closer to achieving your goals. So find out the most suitable communication method, and develop your own style that works best for you.

When you are establishing a business, these core leadership skills will help you excel in positions of entrepreneurship in the most effective ways. The simple way to put them is:

Vision: Allows you to see where you are heading as an entrepreneur.

Strategy building and planning: Gives you the right direction that goes straight toward your goals.

Discernment: Allows you to deal the most unexpected situations in the most effective manner.

Communication: Gives you an opportunity to share your ideas and vision with other people and influence them to keep them motivated.

Commitment: Allows you to stick to the course even in the most difficult times.

Adopting these qualities are essential for becoming a successful entrepreneurial leader.

Chapter 6

Team Building
Entrepreneurship Key to Growth

A large successful business may depend highly on its entrepreneur and it is rarely a one-man show. Name any big organization and there's no way it could be running without a team of dedicated employees. In short, no matter how hard you try, you cannot do it all by yourself.

As an entrepreneur, it is very natural to desire taking the entire business like the lone captain. After all, you are the innovator and idea-generator behind your startup, and it is absolutely natural to feel that no one else except you will understand the goals and visions associated like you.

This could still be possible when you are setting up your business, but if you want your business to scale, controlling every tiny detail all by yourself is not possible.

This chapter will revolve around the importance of building a team for an entrepreneur, and all the aspects associated with it.

The Importance of Working with a Solid Team

Building a strong team with individuals who are as passionate as you are for the business can be quite challenging. Yet, it is a crucial step that you must take if you want your small startup to get off the ground and operate on a large scale. The effort and time you will invest in building your team is definitely going to pay off in the long run.

If you have been planning to do it all by yourself and make your business a one-man show, go through the following reasons why finding the right employees and working with a solid team is a better option for startups.

Constructive Criticism

It is not easy to set up your business, especially if you have no experience. Regardless of how passionate you are about your business or how much you believe in the execution of the idea in your mind, it is just not possible to give yourself the much-required constructive criticism, which is essential to ensure your business is operated and managed in the most efficient possible way.

Even the best business plans can sometimes have unavoidable flaws which can only be rooted and addressed when it undergoes constructive criticism. It is not easy to look at your own business or business idea with that judgment. And therefore, it is important to have a team that works for you to give you better ideas to manage and operate your business much more successfully.

This is the point where a team can help you identify your mistake and work together to finding solutions to those problems. While the control of the business remains in your hand, you know that you have people you can rely to make your business even more perfect. After all, businesses can totally flip between failure and success if only one of the mistakes is corrected.

Expanding Your Work

Expanding the number of employees—in most cases –mean you are expanding your work. Businesses usually do not hire new people just to bring around a bunch of new people to sit in the office. Hiring a team means much more than that. It means having an additional resource to help you with expanding your work as well as with helping you make decisions.

Every individual you are hiring for your business brings their own network with them. Keeping in mind the position these people are hired on, this factor can become highly useful for your business. Indeed, business is more about who you know instead of how you know. In short, expanding your work by hiring a kickass team will allow you to expand your network that eventually works in favor of your business.

While it is possible for an entrepreneur to set up a business on his or her own, compare a single person running around every department and each aspect of entrepreneurship in contrast to skilled people dedicatedly doing the same for their respective departments. Without a doubt, the results will be much better and efficient with the latter setting. In this case, the potential for success is much higher for a business.

Respecting Different Perspective

Working with a team means more people to give ideas to you! There are always multiple ways to tackle with a problem. If you are handling your business alone, you may only be able to see it from a single perspective. You may take certain things into consideration and may miss out on the other important ones. The more ideas you take into consideration the better solution you can find. And this can be achieved when you have more people working for you.

This point is important because regardless of your success as an entrepreneur, you might have a very narrow and particular way to address and solve a problem. You might follow certain strategies and solving tactics and stick to it. This may not always work for you. Sometimes, it is important to strategically come up with multiple ideas that can be put together to find and effective and superior solution.

So build a team who can bump off ideas and help you with decision making when you are stuck in a situation. Work with people who understand the importance of learning and listening to ideas coming from different people.

Working with a solid team can make all the difference in the world to how your business is operating. A top team is a key to growth and success of your business.

The Roles and Responsibilities of Team Working

Even though you may want to, you really cannot do it all yourself! This is especially true if you are looking forward to expanding your business and making it a large, successful company one day. It is important to understand the value of having a strong team. Unless you have some reliable human resource working for you at the top, you and your startup will continue to struggle for success and growth.

It is important to understand the importance, as well as know how to select, manage, and lead a solid team for your business to grow. You may not necessarily have to start with a large team. When you start small, starting alone, or with only a few team members, is okay. However, as you plan to grow your business and expand the operations, you should hire more team members to take care of the areas they are skilled at. In short, it is very important for a business to establish their top team as the business starts to grow.

The team you choose will play a significant role, and therefore it is very important that you are able to select a team that helps you manage the operations, expand your work, and even help you fulfill a part of your leadership responsibilities and roles.

When you have your top team ready, each and every member should be capable of fulfilling the following responsibilities, keeping the interest of your business ahead of everything else.

The head of the departments should be able to:

- Manage their department and functional aspects in the most effective manner. They should be able to utilize the allocated resources effectively for best results.

- Retain and attract new and skilled people to the department for increased productivity and growth.

- Communicate with their subordinates so that every individual in the department is well aware and completely understands the mission, vision, plan, and the values associated with the business. The heads must ensure that all the members in the department are able to relate to the plan in terms of their role in the business so that great results can be expected of them.

The members of the executive team should be able to:

- Be able to manage the idea generation, implementation, and execution of the plan that the company has outlined.

- Become a role model for activities such as problem-solving, teamwork, and innovation.

- Play an active role in the business, and should help other members in the team or their department to achieve their goals for the overall success of the company.

The members of your leadership team should be able to:

- Help the entrepreneur reconstruct the plan for business growth after working on the existing plan and making it better for the company.
- Build and protect a culture within the organization that constantly strives for and supports growth.
- Optimize resources in order to achieve the goals of the company.

Without a doubt, building a solid team is a pivotal part of a successful business. As an entrepreneur, you might face challenges in aligning and building a team of people with diverse skills and mindsets working toward a common goal. However, with the right entrepreneurial leadership qualities, you can surely achieve that.

Facing the Challenge of Changing Team Members

The moment you realize that the team that is working for you is the best team you could have ever imagined, you receive a few resignations. At the same time, you are hiring new people and there comes a time when almost all the old faces are out of the business, and you are left with an entirely new team. In simple words, your company is facing employee turnover where the retention level of the existing employees is low.

Sadly, this could make running business operations smoothly extremely difficult. You have to start everything from the scratch, and all the time you have invested in your previous employees for training has been lost.

So what can be done in such a case? While you cannot really force people to stay or stop hiring people even when you need them, controlling employee turnover rate is the best and most effective solution to this problem. While you can continue to train the new employees you are hiring, you can also retain the current ones and ensure the expertise and experience stays within the business. There are a number of tips on how this can be achieved. You may already be aware of a few of these ways. We will put here some of the most effective ones so you can instantly benefit from them.

- **Hiring people with long-term goals:** Only people with long-term goals are believed to stay longer with you. While there's no such rule here, the pattern is pretty much in the favor of the business. This is something you must judge during the hiring process.

Hiring the right employees with clear goals is the best way to ensure your employees don't leave you midway.

- **Don't keep people who are not a perfect fit for your business:** Don't wait for them to resign; save both your time and training. When you find employees who do not fit in, get rid of them as soon as possible. As it is said, "A stitch in time, saves nine!" Take a proactive approach there.

- **Discuss what favors them:** Instead of talking about everything that interests your business, discuss with employees what interests them. Make sure they are aware that their personal growth and success depends on the growth and success of the company. Therefore, the more they contribute in the success of the business, they more growth they can expect. When the business pays off and recognizes the efforts put in by employees, they remain loyal.

- **Reward employees:** In addition to appreciating and valuing your employees, offer them some real-time awards so that their recognition and contribution toward the company is being celebrated. It is important that you are clear with the reward system. Make it specific and make them loyal to you in the long run.

- **Prioritize employee satisfaction and happiness:** These are the factors that will encourage them to decline a better job opportunity. If an employee is satisfied and happy with you, he or she may reject a higher-paying opportunity. Find out what keeps them happy and satisfied. The environment you provide them with plays a big role, so make sure you work on that too. Invest in the satisfaction and happiness of your employee, and it will pay off in terms of their loyalty to the business.

As an entrepreneur, you are more aware of your employees and their activities. You have a fair idea of what will keep them satisfied with the job and will retain them. So make sure you do everything what helps you keep your employees loyal to you.

Five Important Habits Every Entrepreneur Should Practice

Setting up and establishing a startup business is nothing less than a roller coaster ride. There are both ups and downs down the road. Although most entrepreneurs are already born with the natural qualities of a successful entrepreneur, there are some must-have codes that you need in order to run your business smoothly.

Build Work Ethics

Other than the natural leadership qualities, a successful entrepreneur should also be able to build strong work ethics. These are the pillars that help a business stand strong and run smoothly. Ethics are essential. You need to set them straight to establish your business the right way.

There are various factors that can be combined together to build strong work ethics. First and foremost, your integrity as an entrepreneur is essential for your company, as well as your team members. It is also important to earn more customers and set your business right.

Setting the work ethics will also help you with team management. Your subordinates should rely on you completely, and should be aware of the foundation they should follow. A strong work ethics will keep you moving and will not let your business fall even in the most difficult of times.

Expand

Be productive, as much as you can. It is more important than being busy. That's the way you can expand and establish your business even further. In being an entrepreneur, it is very common for you to go through the "I don't have any time" syndrome. If you are always "too busy" and still fail to achieve your targets, you might not be utilizing your most important and scarce resource: "time" effectively. So instead of being "just busy," try to be more productive so that you can achieve your targets and expand your business as you desire.

Set up a list and prioritize your things to do. No more procrastination!

Don't Be Afraid Of Working with Newbies

The best way to effectively work with newbies is by teaching them how to add value to whatever they do. That's the key to developing and setting up a successful team.

Set the example so that your employees learn from you. With every task you take on, act as if it is extremely valuable to you—regardless of how big or small it is. Do things because there is a purpose or a goal you have set for it, and not only for the sake of it. Prioritize and have the right intention to make everything worth it.

Be Quick

While this is a quality that usually comes from within, if you do not have those efficiently trained and programmed DNAs, you can go ahead and develop it simply by practicing it.

When you are running your own business, you are expected to be quick - in both making a decision, and in implementing it. Don't hesitate in being on your toes—this is something expected of you being an entrepreneur. Break the shell and come out of your comfort zone. Take up tasks you once thought you couldn't do and set a deadline for yourself. Monitor and appreciate your progress.

Passion Is Important

If you don't want to be tired of your business, make sure you indulge into something you are interested in; or better yet, something you are passionate about. The less you treat work as work, and more as a hobby, you will enjoy every bit of it. This will also encourage you to focus on the details, and invest more time and effort into it unless it is as established and big as you have dreamed of.

Last, but not the least, leadership and entrepreneurship is subjective and does not have to follow a pattern. It varies based on the type of business you run. Therefore, it is important that you keep your business, industry, employees, market, and competitors in mind. This will help you make decisions and take actions that are suitable and in favor of your business.

Final Word

Successful entrepreneurs have various habits and qualities that they attribute to the success of their business. Taking it up as an inspiration and copying some of the most successful and common habits can instantly increase your chances to be successful once you have decided to give up your job and become an entrepreneur.

An entrepreneur manages and organizes a business with a lot of risk and instability into account. This is one of the most important qualities that make them what they are. So if you have finally decided to go after your passion. and give up the 9 to 5 routine you constantly feel you are not made for, then go ahead and live your dream and become an entrepreneur.

This book has everything you need to learn about entrepreneurship and how to get into the business. Make the most out of the information shared here and get started to make your dreams come true.

Good luck!

ENTREPRENEURSHIP
THE WRIGHT WAY

www.ingramcontent.com/pod-product-compliance
Lightning Source LLC
Chambersburg PA
CBHW060350190526
45169CB00002B/557